Escaping a past

Tony Snow

 pencil

ISBN 978-93-5458-972-0
© Tony Snow 2021
Published in India 2021 by Pencil

A brand of
One Point Six Technologies Pvt. Ltd.
123, Building J2, Shram Seva Premises,
Wadala Truck Terminal, Wadala (E)
Mumbai 400037, Maharashtra, INDIA
E connect@thepencilapp.com
W www.thepencilapp.com

Author biography

I had written this book about15 years ago but not having a lot of knowledge on how computers worked I lost the only copy when my computer died,

Struggling from mental illness from a past that includes murder, drugs, abuse, bribes, cops, stolen cars, dodgy landlords and houses that should have been condemned,I somehow make it through to becoming an author, I want to state that this was my biggest challenge and I slowly got better,

This book was written for a lot of reasons one it was to help me put it all down on paper so I could run through the processes of what I had been through

and try and put it all into prospective another reasons for writing this book was to also help other people who are out there looking for a way out to know that there is light out there even if you can't see it and I'm not talking about a heavenly light or God light or anything like that its more that sometimes we all can get into a dark spot in our lives and it's in those dark moments that we need to know that there is hope even when you can't see it this book was also written for my family and friends so they can better understand me and where I have come from, it was also written for my step children overseas so they might understand just how hard it was for me, before we first ever talked and since me and their mother split this book was written for me, also as someone like me could not ever write let alone a book and disclose all of his wardrobe for the world to see but along the way I have lost friends and loved ones I do have regrets but they are mine and they are something that can only be my burden even though I have shared some of them here, I also need to say that there is plenty more of this story but I could only tell so much of it otherwise no one would want to read it as it would just be to long' I would also like to thank a very few close friends and family for sticking by me when most have fallen by the way side I would like to thank and in no particular order these people who are not just my family and friends but I consider them to be family some blood and some not nevertheless here they are Leanne, Brent, Mikayla, Tom, Jerica, Sandra, Adam, Amanda, Alex, Patricia, Sally, Kylie, Raymond,

You have all been an inspiration to me I thank you from the deepest part of my heart for your love and support that I have had over the years I would not be here today without your kind words and support I have known some of you longer than others but you all hold a special place in my heart as my family as you have all helped me find my way and helped me define who I truly am, I did have some pretty dark days but that is behind me now all I see is a bright future ahead of me.

CONTENTS

Epigraph

A wise Snow once said to me this one line and I've always remembered it.

Events take place due to the fortuitous intersections of decoupled causal chains.

This = "Shit Happens"

Acknowledgements

My Dedication

I would like to thank the following people, in no particular order, for their part in my journey so far. It has been a long and winding road. I care deeply for each of you and thank you so much more than you may realise. You have all contributed to me becoming me - the man I am today.

To my partner: Thank you for the ongoing support all the time we have been together. You found me with my heart pretty beaten up by past events. My head was such a mess too. I did my best to hide it, I think. It was you who put me back together, slowly but surely. Every day you brought me out of a dark, tight spot. I have had so many inner struggles while writing this book, Escaping a Past, and you have encouraged me the whole way. You are my rock and my safe place. Without you, this book would not have been written once, and definitely not twice! It has been long ride with a few bumps along the way but it is finished at last. I appreciate and love you so much.

I would like to give special thanks to my friend who has done the editing of my book. Without your input, it would have never have gotten off the ground. You have done an amazing job with it. You know my difficulties with spelling and such, though I love to write. If I had tried to hand write it no-one would be able to read it, not even me! The first time I wrote Escaping a Past I lost the whole book when my computer died, then I left it for years before attempting to write it again a second time. Again, thank you for your support and advice over the years. It means a lot to me that we are good friends.

I would love to give a big shout out to two very dear friends of mine from America. You have always been there for me for a very long time now. You know who you are; I wrote about you on the first page of this book. You are both very special to me. You have known the real struggles I have had over the years and I thank you sincerely. I love you guys more than you know. We don't get to talk so much now but I think of you every day. Life just gets busy sometimes but I don't love you any less, that's for sure. Thank you for being my mates. It means the world to me that you are still in touch. Love you guys!

I know a lot of the people who truly know me will say "This is crazy! Why even bother?" but I would like to thank my ex-wife for giving me a reason to take the risk and get out of my captivity. It was more than just risky, but I faced it for the sake of love. If I had not fallen in love with you I might still be there, as stupid as that makes me sound. No matter what the cost was to me and my heart when it ended, I truly thank you, more deeply than you know. I don't regret anything. I forgive you from the bottom of my heart and hold no remorse or anger towards you. You have a special place in my heart, filled with memories of happy times. They are locked away, but I won't forget. May the rest of your life bring you happiness and joy.

I thank my five step-children, here and overseas. I hate the word "step"; I always felt like your father and that's how I have always treated you guys. I think of you as my own and I am one lucky father to have you all in my life! I have not been able to have biological children and I don't feel like I have missed out; I am blessed and so grateful that you let me be part of your life too. To the five of you: I love you all so dearly. Over the years you have made me cry and laugh and made me so proud of you! A large part of who I am today has been shaped by you. I love you all from the bottom of my heart and I always will.

Thank you, K&R, for being my mates over the years. Thank you for taking me in when I came back from overseas; I had nothing. It will always mean so much to me. Thank you again!

I would also like to thank people that I hold dear to me, deep in my heart. People that are no longer with us but made such a difference. Thanks to my Uncle for helping to make me the man I am today. He was the only real man I had in my life when I was growing up, a man I still look up to today. You have been gone for a long time. I still model myself on you, trying to be kind and gentle and live up to what you showed me. You always knew how to make me smile. Thank you for the memories.

I would like to thank my best mate for getting me out of that crazy ass environment. You have to help yourself before others step in to help you, and you stepped in just at the right moment. I sent you a text and you got the ball rolling in less than a week. The escape happened but without you I might still be there, taking each day as it came and praying for a miracle. You bought the airline ticket and gave me a place to stay when I finally got away. We have been mates for more than thirty years and I thank you so much for all your support and treating me like a brother.

You may wonder at this, but I am thanking a dog! She's not an ordinary dog at all. Thank you, Jesse. When I got you, your name was Sophie but never suited you so I changed it. I thank you for being the best dog friend a man could ever have. You knew me so well; you knew what I wanted without me having to say it. We had a very special bond. No other dog will ever take your place. I love you.

A big thank you to one of my first cousins. At the time I was finishing my book, she was battling hard with cancer. Thank you for letting me raise money in your name for cancer research so other people and their families don't have to go through what you have been through. You have now passed away. What a beautiful soul you are! May you rest in peace.

Thank you to my Italian friend for painting Jesse for me. It was done while I was writing the last part of this book. She told me "I'll paint her, then she will always watch over you while you sleep." What a beautiful, kind thing you have done for me. I only had one photo of Jesse; you truly did her justice.

Deep gratitude to one of my heroes, John Cena. His saying is "Never give up." I believe in his strength and I've always loved his hustle, loyalty and respect. Remembering him and how he is has helped me to stay strong when life was at its hardest. So thank you, John. I know you hear it all the time, and no wonder. You are a great role model for children as well as adults all over the world.

Elon Musk is another one who gives me the strength to know better days are ahead. With the way he took huge risks with his rockets, He never gave up even after the first second and third rocket exploded he puts it all on the line for the forth rocket which was a huge win, I respect his tenacity, The way he thinks and the way he goes about running his car company and last on this list is wanting us to become a two planet society, Elon is a very smart man and one man in the future I hope to meet to shake his hand and to sit for ten minutes at least and just listen to him talk, Every time I hear him I stop what I am doing and I listen hard what a great man.

Isaac Butterfield, YouTube sensation, Comedian and all round nice guy, One of the few that I love to watch, He is also someone that had it hard and come through a ruff childhood and how he used laughter to not just become a comedian but a funny one at that, I love that he is not scared to take on any topic and tell you how it is through laughter and the choice of words that he uses to capture his audience.

This is a hard one. I don't even know your name. I was walking one day and you pulled over and gave me a lift, saying "I can tell you are carrying a huge weight on your shoulders by the way you are walking." You were right. I told you I was getting a divorce. You gave me the gift of your wisdom and good words to strengthen me. I thank you for your decency, for noticing and picking me up. I was in a bad way.

Corey Taylor, an author, song writer and lead singer of two bands is another one of my heroes. One of his bands, Stone Sour, is one of my favourite bands of all times. He writes amazing lyrics. I love how he tells it straight, no bullshit. That drew me to his books; I have read them all and loved every one of them. I can hear the truthfulness in his singing and it was part of what inspired me to write my book a second time. There is no one like him. Thank you, Corey, and keep rocking.

Another of my musical heroes is Lemmy from Motörhead. You passed away a few years ago, but you helped me through a lot of hard times. Your style of music inspired me and your saying, "Live to win, die to lose", held me steady in time of great need. May you rock God's socks off and show Him how it's done. Your music pulled me out of many depressed states. Thank you for who you were. You never conformed to anybody's standards but your own. I, too, am no sheep. Thank you.

I would love to thank the music artists for giving me the pleasure of listening, escaping reality and escaping the past. Not in any order of preference, thanks to Madchild, AC/DC, Motörhead, Tom MacDonald, Nova, Rose Tattoo, Stone Sour, Iron Maiden, The Cult, Monster Magnet, Doro Peach, Divinyls, Shannon Noll, Judas Priest and Gums N Roses – just to name a few.

Ned Kelly is one of my Australian heroes. I love his strength, his dedication to his family and his constant struggle with the law. I knew that feeling when I was younger. I respect Ned for being a gentleman with women and children. I follow the wisdom behind his saying "Such is life." Sometimes there is nothing I can do to change things and the only way to inner peace is acceptance. Such is life.

I would like to give the last thank you to myself for keeping ongoing when it was all bleak, inside and out. I almost gave up on everything a few times but I didn't. I've had a great crew behind me – all of the people mentioned above. Thank you. I love you all more than I can ever express. You are very special to me; I am grateful for all the support you have given me over the years we have known each other.

Chapter 1 The Begining

A young boy, at the tender age of 5, is struggling to understand why his own mother would beat him. Not just a smack on the bottom for being a naughty boy, but a vicious flogging.

Why would she take to me with a long piece of garden hose? It did not matter if I was good or bad, only her mood determined whether I would get a beating or not. I felt terrible pressure, and a burning desire to ask "Why Mummy, what are you hitting me for?" and yell "Mummy, I did not do that!" "Mummy, that hurts!" but there were no answers – only further abuse. The hose was only used on me – and, I found out later, one other – but that unspeakably cruel punishment was never used on my older or younger brothers.

On the day that this started, I tried to escape the harshest part of this treatment. I was told to chop some wood with a tomahawk, kindling to get the fire started. Mom watched me from the top of the ramp at the back of the house. It was an old concrete ramp that I used to ride my green plastic racing car down. I felt proud that she had asked me to chop some wood like a man would, but I was only five.

I felt good. I picked up the tomahawk and swung it with all my might. The head of it hit the log very hard. As I lifted the handle to pull it out, I found that the head was stuck deep in the wood. I pulled and heaved, but there was no way it was coming free. I could hear my mum screaming like a mad woman, telling me to stop being silly and get on with it. I said, "Mummy, I can't! It's stuck!" She kept yelling, then said "If you can't pull it out, I'm going to fucking flog your ass until it bleeds!"

I started to panic when I saw Mum go inside the house. I had fear in my heart, dread in my soul, and somehow I knew something bad was about to happen.

There was a very loud bang – it was the back door, swung open so hard that it almost came off the hinges. I looked up There is Mum, with a knife in her hand. She walked down the ramp slowly, taking her time. She looked over at me, staring at me in a way I had never seen before. She glared like she was on a mission from God… or something.

She kept walking slowly to the right hand side of the house. I saw her reach for something, but I did not know what it was. I could see her arm going backward and forwards like she was cutting something. She stopped after a minute or so, and then turned to walk over to me, clearly wanting to freak me out. Mum lifted her hand above her head to show me a piece of green and lighter green pipe – a piece of garden hose she had cut. She said sternly, "I told you I was going to fucking flog you".

Mum told me to turn around and drop my shorts to the ground, but before I even got them down to my ankles, she grabbed the back of my head and whacked me as hard as she could. I could feel the sting and the burn of it, it was so hard and so hot and so bad. I got at least 12 lashes before she shoved me out of the way and told me to stop "crying like a girl and get inside before I do it again".

I ran like a rabbit through the back door, past the dining room and into the door on the left. I stayed there for an hour or so before Mum came into my room. She stood in the doorway with a black shoelace all tied up in knots. She threw it at me, and said "Don't move from that bed until all the knots are undone". I started to undo them, not understanding why she would even give this to me.

I undid them all slowly, and when I finished I left it on my bed and walked out of my room. I could hear her voice, which helped me make up my mind what to do, 100%. "The fucking next time I tell you to do something and you don't I'm going to fucking flog you to within an inch of your life". The all I could hear was mumbling and ranting. I could not make the words out after that; what she was saying was all muffled and under her breath. I walked back into my room and sat on the bed. At that moment, I did not feel the pain that was across my lower back, bottom and legs.

I had only just sat on the bed, and I could hear her stomping up the hallway towards my room. Mum walked in. She saw the shoelace and looked at me as if she could kill me. Then she slowly came over and grabbed it – and walked out. I lay down, and before I knew it an hour had passed. I was laying on my single bed, the old metal type with springs that always make a loud noise when I moved on it.

I peeked out of my room, ever so quietly. I walked through the dining room to the lounge room that was straight ahead. I could see my mother; she was fast asleep in the lounge chair, with that hose peeking over the top of the arm of the chair. I walked ever so quickly and quietly to the back door, closing it softly behind me. Then I ran down the ramp, up the left side of the house and out to the front gate. I opened the old cast iron gate, and then ran up the road to a friend's house. It was half a street away, but thankfully only that far as I was out of breath by the time I got there.

The house was quiet – no cars in the drive, but I knocked on the front door anyway. I waited and listened. No answer. Then I walked up the driveway towards their back door. I looked around. It was so quiet, but I knew it was possible someone was there, so I knocked on the back door. No answer. I was bewildered now; all hope was gone.

I knew I could not be spotted, so I started to walk off. I did not know where I was going, but saw a small door on the side of the house, where people store lawn mowers. I had myself a great idea! I could hide there until my friend came home. I knew I had to hide from her brutal punishment.

I was scared because it was so dark inside, but I was not going to be found by mother dear, so without hesitation I climbed inside. It was very dark, but I did feel safe now. I found a piece of cardboard just inside the door, so I laid my head down on that old flattened box. I thought to myself "I am so sore, so tired…." Soon I was fast asleep.

When I woke up, I knew that I was going to be in even more trouble if my friend was not at home. I climbed back out the way I went in and again I knocked on the front door and on the back door. No one home. I was so tired and so hungry and it was getting on dark. I started down the driveway heading to the left and then the right towards my house. I thought it would be smart to walk on the grass strip in the middle of the driveway and be quiet, but I looked up and there was a police car!

I thought "Wow, this car is so cool!" It was a HQ Holden and I so wanted to go for a drive with the sirens on! I looked over to my right, and at the front of my house was Mum and two police officers, a lady and a man. The man was in charge. He told Mum I had better be punished good. When they left, she decided a good punishment was a whole plate of beetroot, that I had to eat before I went to bed. I hated beetroot so much! I suppose Mum knew that.

I screwed my face up and made moaning sounds so that maybe my Mum would say "You've had enough, boy, just go to bed", but that never came. I ate every little bit. I did not want a repeat of the day's earlier events. My bum, lower back and legs hurt so bad.

I went to bed after a long lecture on how I must do as I am told, and that this would be the outcome every time if I did something wrong: first up, a flogging; second up, a whole plate of beetroot and third, a nice long lecture if I did not eat the whole plateful.

I went to bed sore and hungry. Her bullying made my ears hurt, too.

Chapter 2 Bad Start

My mother got with this man. That wound up being the second bad and sad part of this story. My step father was an old army type of guy, very strict in his beliefs. It was his way or the highway.

To be honest, I was not the brightest boy when I was younger. I remember him telling me one time that I would end up in jail by the time I was 18, because I did not show enough respect to carry myself in public. What he said seemed to have something to do with my sleeves being rolled up, not down. That was a little confusing to me.

He had hair like Elvis, shiny black, with sideburns to match. He always wore slacks, never shorts, and a long sleeved shirt. The sleeves were firmly buttoned down. And he always wore a tie.

He chose the perfect attire for a man who liked to hide what he was really like. He wanted to be able to pick on people without others seeing it. It worked. Everyone thought he was a good guy, a man's man. Tall and clean cut, he drank with the lads and slapped his partner around. It was puzzling to me, how nice clothes equalled good reputation.

Less than a handful of people knew the truth. He was a control freak who seemed to feel like a man only when he beat my mother and me if we did not do as we were told. For him, there was nothing quite like throwing the plates across the room if dinner was not what he wanted, or the mashed potato was not just right, or it was cold because he was running late after he decided to stay at the pub to have another round of beers with the boys. I guess that was all our fault? Nothing made sense.

I never knew if it was my fault that my mother would always pick on me, and never my brothers. Neither of them had ever copped the hose, let alone a smack on the bum with a bare hand. God forbid they might be disciplined for being naughty! My older brother was a goodie two-shoes, Mummy's golden boy. The youngest son was her angel.

That damn hose. It would sit beside the arm chair, waiting for my mistakes, or the mistakes of my two brothers. I wore the lashes on my back, as well as my legs and face and bum as I grew from a little boy to a young man. I was still in trouble most days for not doing as I was told.

I had a hard time understanding why my brothers could do the same as me or worse, and there would be no punishment for them. But I deserved to be beaten to within an inch of my life with a garden hose if I did not get my brothers BMX bike for him before I went to school. Does it sound like the punishment fit the crime?

My step father bossed me around, always telling me I was a loser and that someday I would end up in jail. This wannabe Father of the Year gambled away a fortune on the dogs and the horses and at the Casino. Would they call him a good man if they could see how he would bash my Mum around with his closed fists, or how he always got drunk at our house and lay around with a can of VB or a can of beer on his stomach? He never gave her money to look after his first and only son. What sort of man does that make him?

He would turn up late at night drunk. His place was too far away to walk, and he could not drive drunk. He would kick and bash on the door for hours. One night, he must have thought, "How will I get their attention? I'll throw bricks on the roof!" And he did. Another time, he took our car and drove home drunk. I would hide in my room, waiting for him to go to sleep. He was totally unpredictable. I never knew what he would do to me.

On my 16th birthday, my uncle gave me a sock full of coins. Both my brothers got a sack to buy me something, because it was my birthday. My little brother saw what I had, and he wanted it. Mum said I had to give it to him, otherwise I was "going to get a flogging". "Why should I?" I said. "It's my birthday present from my uncle to me!" As she began to open her mouth to say it again, I saw her heading for the chair. I knew what she was up to. I ran with that full sock and gave it to my younger brother. When I turned to shout out to her that I'd given him my money, there she was with that hose in her right hand. She was hitting her left hand softly, telling me that I was a lucky boy that I had given over what she had asked.

The last big sad day before my life changed forever was Christmas day, 1985. We all got up to open our presents. I was not over-excited, because my two brothers were spoilt all the time, and I knew the focus would be on them. Life was not any different on this day. My older brother got clothes and money and Star Wars figures, to replace the ones that I gave away. He had stolen my money, for whatever reason, so I got him back by giving them all away at school.

My younger brother then opened his presents. He got a remote-controlled car, the one that I wanted. Mum knew that I wanted it so bad. He got a brand new BMX Road King bike, and clothes. Then it was my turn. I got a black Kenworth truck with a cord attached to it. I had to walk about a foot behind it – that's not a real remote-controlled truck. I was told that there was a special present for me in the boot of the HD Holden Kingswood, but I would get it later. No clothes or money.

Lunch was ready then, and we had to have it while it was hot. i could smell the roast chicken with roast vegetables, carrots and potatoes. We sat down and said the Lord's Prayer. No one was allowed to talk but my step-father. He ranted and raved about himself, how he did such a good job looking after everyone for Christmas, with money and presents and food. I could not believe what I was hearing. He crapped on and on and on about himself…

After lunch, he took me to the car and opened the boot. I feasted my eyes on…two broken BMX's. One was just a rusty black frame, with a crank and pedals, no neck or fork. The other was a rusty girl's bike frame, red, badly cracked. The handle bars, forks, neck wheels and chains all came off that one and I had to put the parts on the other frame.

That was a pretty shitty Christmas, even by the normal miserable standard. I didn't ask for anything special – just a normal BMX bike. I did not want a fancy one like my brother's, but he got new one and I had to tear down two old rusted bikes to try to make a whole one. But I did it! And by myself, I might add.

Not too many months after that dismal Christmas, it all went downhill again. March 26th, 1986, was the fateful day that Mum just could not take it anymore. After years of mental and physical thrashings I suppose that stabbing him was her only way out of the mess.

I was now a young man. Just before this showdown, I found myself a place to be free of all that fighting and misery, in an old but welcoming house. I could stay off the streets and just have a smoke and not witness the horror of everyday life at home. It was a carefree place, filled with strange people, which became the next step for me, a young man wanting to escape my past.

I had come home from my refuge to find nothing unusual going on. I saw Mum in the kitchen. She told me my stepfather was very drunk and abusive as normal, and when she brought him back from the pub I had to pretty much disappear. The phone rang; it was him, drunk as a skunk. He told her he had "a bone to pick" with me – I was the target this time. She went and picked him up from the pub and brought him home.

The first thing he did as soon as he got in the door was to come and look for me. I could hear him saying "Where is that little cunt?" I was hiding in the bathroom. He came in and picked me up from behind, with his hands in my armpits, shoving me hard and kicking me in my behind. Just to add to the mess, he shoved my head into the wall. When I recovered enough to go into the lounge room to help my Mum, they had already started to fight. He smacked her around the face with an open hand at first. She punched him right back with a closed fist. He shouted, "I'm going to kill that little cunt! I need to teach him respect!" They traded a few more blows. I walked into the kitchen, scared. I watched the fight, feeling helpless. I was stuck in one spot, so stricken with fear that I could not move. That is what held me back.

Now my stepfather was hurling abuse at my Mum, calling her a weak cunt. In return, she said "If you don't fuck off, I will slice you with a knife!" He called her a weak bitch, and said she did not have the balls to go through with it. With that, Mum ran into the kitchen to get a knife to defend herself from his fists. They began punching each other again and yell, and he sneered "See, I told you that you don't have the balls". She swung, and sliced him across the belly. He called her a weak fucking bitch, then walked off to clean himself up. I could hear him rambling on and swearing his head off. He came back out after a few minutes, and hit her again. My younger brother jumped in front of them both. "Stop hitting Mum!". His father back-handed him, and he ran off screaming.

I was still frozen with fear. Mum kicked my step-father in the balls and he went down. That gave Mum time to go look for my brother. She came back after a few minutes and started in on him, saying "Now look what you have done! My youngest son is gone!". He shouted out "You can all go to hell! He was no man to stand up to me! I am his father!". Mum said "You are not a father's asshole!". He called her a weak bitch and punched her again.

 She stabbed him in the chest, and he went down like a sack of spuds.

He got up and walked outside, then collapsed on the stairs at the back door. Mum screamed out for me to hold him while she made the call for an ambulance. He looked at me, pointed his index finger in my face and said "I'm going to get you, boy!". And then he passed out.

Mum went to jail. My little brother went into foster care because he was only 10. The older brother moved away. I had no place to go but that old house with strange people in it. Even though I knew the couple who lived there, I did not want to impose on them. There was a new woman in that house, who was a friend of theirs. My second downfall began when I met her.

Chapter 3 Bad Memories

Looking back, there were many days like that in my childhood. Most of my life, there had been some form of abuse going on, physical or mental. Physically, I was hit with a garden hose, thrown into walls and punched about the head. Mentally, I was tricked and blamed and told, in so many ways, that I was no good.

One time that really stands out for me happened when I was seven. My younger brother had gotten into a whole packet of crayons. It would have been fine if Mum was looking after him, but no, it was the monster himself. I have had so many bad dreams over the years because of him, and this story is nearly the same as all the others. The way abuse turned toward me, I felt like I must be the Devil's spawn. They seemed to think they had to beat the Devil out of me.

That day, as usual, my stepfather was deeply engaged in his afternoon ritual – laying on the couch with a Victoria Bitter glass stubby beer bottle on his stomach, while he listened to the afternoon horse races. Race Four was on the radio. He always listened to this, treating it as his most important occupation. I never interrupted him, because if I did he would lose his cool and slap me about.

Not long after the race was finished, he got up to go to the toilet. A few minutes later, he went to check on my younger brother, his son. My brother had scribbled over part of the darkish cream wall with crayons. He yelled out for me to get a bucket of water and a sponge. I got those things together from under the sink in the laundry, and without wasting any time I rushed them to him. He snatched them off me like a child grabbing a toy. He looked at me and said "Boy, clean this fucking mess up. Call out for me when you're done." I said 'Yes, sir" as he walked away.

I started on the wall while he went back to his beer and horse races. I scrubbed and scrubbed, but no matter what direction I moved the sponge, it did not come off. It was smearing and smearing so I closed my eyes and scrubbed with all my might, hoping that when I opened them it would be gone. I scrubbed left and right and up and down and even in circles. I counted down from 10 to zero in my mind – 10 9 8 7 6 5 4 3 2 1 0. I opened my eyes, and to my horror it looked really bad, much worse than it had before. Red, blue, green and orange were smeared into a swirling pattern. It truly looked like someone had thrown up all over the wall.

I started to panic. I did not know what to do. I was not going to call out to him, as I knew it was not going to have a good outcome. Suddenly he shouted out from the lounge room, "Are you done yet, boy?" I said "No, sir." I was lost and bewildered and devastated, to tell you the truth.

I did not know what else to do, so I sat down on the floor and played with my little brother. He was playing with two of his Matchbox toy cars. One was a yellow 1957 Chevy and the other was a 1969 Dodge Charger, the same one that was in the Dukes of Hazard, only green. We played like what seemed forever. It was a good memory that I am fond of today.

All of a sudden I could hear him coming down the hall. He screamed out "Is it off the wall yet, boy?" I said, "No, sir". I jumped to my feet. All I could hear was him shouting "Fuck! Fuck! Fuck!! little boy! Do you know my horse has come in last? Of course I had a bet on it! It was a sure winner!" He had put $200 on a long odds horse and now I could hear his drunk ass crashing into the lounge room wall. Bang! Crash! Now he's hitting the hallway wall and then standing before me, looking at the mess that I had made much worse.

He looked at me with so much hatred that I closed my eyes. I did not want to see what would come next. I felt his big rough builder's hands grab my ears, squeezing so tight that I was screaming for him to let me go. I begged him to let go of my ears. Suddenly, he picked me up from behind while he still had hold of me by the ears. He started to bang my head into the wall, swearing the whole time. "Fuck this!" Bang! "Fuck you!" Bang! "You are nothing but a lazy dumb fuck!" Bang! Bang! "It's your fault I lost all that money!" Bang! "You will end up in jail, you lazy good for nothing!" Bang! Bang! "You made such a fucking mess!" Bang! Bang! Bang! And then I passed out.

When I woke, I was aching so much that I felt like my head would burst. I was a used, broken toy that he no longer wanted. I lay there on the cold floor. I did not know if five minutes had passed, or hours. Then Mum walked in, shopping in hand.

She saw me laying on the floor. For the first time, she protected me. She ran into the lounge room where he was proudly laying down again, beer on his stomach and radio blasting. "What the fuck is wrong with you?" she screamed at him. "Why is my son laying on the floor with bruises all around his head and face?" Then she started to punch into him, screaming even louder "What did you do to my son?" He managed to get to his feet and punched her right back. Her only safe move was to just kick him so hard in the nuts that he fell to the ground, sobbing like a baby. Then she kicked him in the stomach and walked off screaming at the top of her lungs "Don't you ever touch my son again!"

Mum attended to me and for once, I saw a mother's love. She picked me up and told me everything was going to be alright. Little did I know, it was all just a lie.

Mum managed to clean the wall. I don't know how she did it, but you would never have known what had happened. That night was so strange. Not a word was spoken at the dinner table until I asked if I could leave the table. I had eaten all my food – mashed potatoes, carrots, beans and sausages. She said "Yes. You can go to your room, but make sure you wash your hands and brush your teeth." I said "Yes, Mum" as I left the table.

I went to the bathroom and washed my hands and brushed my teeth. I looked in the mirror and saw that the top of my head had lots of bruises, blue and purple. I was horrified that I looked like some monster out of a Star Wars movie, or like the Hunchback of Notre Dame. I went to bed. I tried to get some sleep, because I knew that it would be just me and my older brother at home in the morning.

When I woke the next day, my mother, step-father and younger brother had already gone. I remember his car, a mustardy coloured 1969 HT Holden Kingswood. Me and my brother were left behind. We made Weet-bix, four! with milk and a sprinkle of sugar for breakfast. We started talking about what we could do so it wouldn't be such a boring day.

My brother said maybe I could wash Mum's car. I said I would get it all ready to wash. I was lucky the car was under the carport; it was a very warm day. My brother had the bucket and a sponge and told me he had put the good stuff in it. I started to wash the car, A 1964 EH Holden wagon. It was light green with a white roof, stock, a lovely old car. In later years, I would own three. I washed and scrubbed, top to bottom. I was a little concerned when I finished rinsing it off, as the body of the car was very shiny, and all the windows had a strange film over them. I asked my brother about this, But he informed me that the car was clean and that was what it was supposed to look like. I was happy with that.

It was not long before our mother came home, and as soon as I heard the car in the driveway I ran to it in great excitement. I wanted my mother to be proud of me and my hard work. I started to stutter, which I always did when I got excited, so I grabbed her hand and took her to see her car. My mother looked at the car. Such a look is not good. She asked me "What the fuck did you wash the car with?" I said just a bucket with water and a sponge and some special stuff my brother put in the bucket for me. She screamed out his full name, and when she did this you knew she was not happy.

My older brother came out and said "What, Mummy?" She said, "What did you put in this bucket?" He said, "I did not put anything in the bucket, Mummy, he wanted to wash the car on his own, I did not put nothing in the bucket Mummy, I swear Mummy, I seen him grab that glass bottle off the shelf and pour it into the water." Next thing I felt was a backhand across the face. "You stupid boy! Go to your room!"

I thought I was doing a nice thing for my mother, but my brother just played me for a fool. He put a half a litre bottle of motor oil into the bucket with a little water, just to get me in trouble again. It took a while before I could see this pattern.

I went to my room and waited for the next piece of shoelace to untie.

Chapter 4 More Of The Same

By the time I was 15, I had seen more than 100 lashings with that hose. I was slapped in the face and sent to bed without food more times than I could count. After all those years, the hose needed some repair with electrical tape – it was beginning to fray at the ends, and beginning to split. I could see the blue tip sticking out of my Mum's chair. It hurt just the same as always.

I had a great idea! It just popped into my head. I thought "I will take that damned hose and throw it away!" No more abuse! I grabbed it when Mum was making dinner and I ran out the front door, up the street and threw it in the long grass at the park. It was far enough from the house that I knew my Mum would never find it.

I was so proud of myself! I was chuffed! I went straight home as I knew that dinner would not be far away. I walked in the back door just as dinner was being served. Fish fingers with bread and butter, one of my favourites when I was a teenager because it was easy to make. My elder brother was not at home yet.

We were all sitting at the table when the phone rang. It was my brother, asking if he could stay at a friend's place for the night. Mum said "No, I want you home tonight, please." My brother said "Get fucked" and hung up. He knew he would not get into any kind of trouble. When he hung up on her, I could see Mum was so angry she was about to burst, but she said nothing. We all finished our meal, and I washed my hands, brushed my teeth and went to bed.

The next day I went to my friend's place for a few hours. He invited me to stay, so I rang my Mum to let her know. She said "No, just come home." I had a good idea – I just hung up. I thought "Well, my bother gave her the F word and hung up and did not get into trouble. It should be pretty safe". I stayed at my friend's house, and we had fun watching VHS movies and playing board games. The next day, I had cornflakes and milk and a sprinkle of sugar for breakfast, and decided it was time to go home.

Mum was in the laundry, hand washing the clothes. We did not have a washing machine that worked – only an old twin tub that could spin, but not wash. My step father was too tight with his money to buy us what we needed to live comfortably as a family. He preferred gambling it away on the dogs and horses.

She spoke as soon as I walked in the door. "Go to your room!" I did as I was told. "Where is that damned hose?" "What the fuck…?" I thought. I said "I don't know, Mum." All I could hear was Mum slamming doors in the kitchen BANG! Then I heard the back door BANG! and after a few minutes, the back door again - BANG! My bed was facing the door to the hallway. When I looked up, I could see her stomping down the hall toward my room, a new piece of hose in her hand.

I jumped up and slammed the door, and sat with my back against it to keep myself safe. My Mother began to bash on the door. "Let me the fuck in or I'm going to fucking flog you ten times harder and ten times longer!" There was nothing I could do but just sit there and wait. She called out for my older brother to take the door down. As she waited for him to get to the bedroom, I jumped to my feet and ran to the window. I unlocked it and climbed down the big pine tree that grew there. I ran as fast as my legs could carry me to a vacant block of land down the road. A concrete foundation of some kind had been built there a long time ago. All that was left was a slab, two walls and a lid, covered with blackberry bushes. The lid was on ground level, a roof for the space below.

I hid there for quite some time, trying to figure out what to do. I knew I was not old enough to move out on my own, and I would have to return to the place that was Hell itself to me.

On my return, she was waiting in her chair with her trusty new hose. She asked me to be truthful with her and tell her what I had done with the hose. "If you tell me the truth, I will not punish you." I hesitated a few seconds before answering "Yes Mum, I took it and threw it away. Being hit with that thing hurts more than you could ever know". She said "Well, you little fucking cunt, you are getting a flogging, because you took my hose when it was not yours to take; you didn't come home when I asked you to; and you walked out when you knew you had to be punished for everything."

She stood up, and before she could say another word, I said "Mum, he never got into any trouble for telling you to get nicked! He hung up in your face! I just hung up." She started to scream "Don't bring your older brother into this! You did wrong! Don't blame other for your fuck-ups!" She lifted her hand with the hose, and went to swing it.

I did something I never thought I would do, maybe because I was older, maybe because I had had enough of the abuse. I grabbed her around both hands and squeezed and squeezed. They were very small compared to mine. She yelled at me to let go, but I said "No! Not unless you are going to stop hitting me! I am sick of being hit with that hose!" After a few minutes, she promised not to hit me with the hose again. I let her go. I was not sure if I trusted her, but she was my mother, after all.

Later, I wrote in my journal: Battered and bruised, longing for answers that were not forthcoming, asking why as I cried and sobbed. All I saw was rage against me, a child.

I would hide away from the shame. No one really lived like me, I thought, until I grew to be a man and saw many children just like me, battered and bruised, looking for answers that would never come. I see a broken nose, multiple bruises, welts and lashes from a garden hose on a timid child hiding away in my own soul. That child was me. My own mother and step-father hurt me. I still don't have the answers, and now I never will, but I know that it is not right to hurt a child and never was or will be. It is unforgivable to use violence to try to have your own way, to control another person like a puppet on a string. They

will finally grow up, and have no more to do with you in
your life, but terrible damage has been done.

Memories are like coloured, broken, stained glass

Many broken pieces, the shades and colours cracked.

Daydreaming in school is all I can do,

Growing up wondering why my mother is so cruel.

Hate is a strong word.

I can't think of any other way to say it.

Hate has left me with scars; some have never healed.

I have walked through this life fighting, tooth and nail

I've come close to quitting a few times

Not sure how I made it through

All I know is never giving up

Life is like a roller coaster Up and down.

Chapter 5 Long Nights

After all the ruckus, I decided I had had enough. It was time to run away again. The violence and screaming overwhelmed me. I desperately needed some peace and quiet to heal my mind. But I did not get it this time.

I thought to myself "I'll leave tonight when the whole house is asleep." I had to wait until Mum was in bed. I always knew when she was in bed because the television was off, and the whole house was quiet. I lay in my bed, waiting and waiting. I could clearly hear "Hey, Hey, It's Saturday" because the lounge room door was always open, and so was my bedroom door.

"I can't waste any time" I thought, so I kept going over my plan of escape. I heard the television go silent and I knew that it would not be long before I could take off. "Just wait until her door is shut." Click! The door was shut. "Give her another 20 minutes, and then I am out of here!" I told myself. Next time I looked at the clock it was 10:59. "I must have had a nap, but it's ok. Do it now!"

I got out of my bed very slowly, determined not to make a sound. I walked to her door and opened it ever so quietly. I was shocked to see my mother naked, sitting on top of my step-father. I knew they were having sex. He held her by the breasts and she was moaning loudly. "This is perfect!" I thought. I had to be very, very quiet after closing Mum's door again, because my little brother slept in the same room as I did.

I could not leave until I had packed some food. I went to the pantry and loaded my school bag with tins of baked beans, some choc chip cookies, a few tins of sardines and two packets of Snakes.

The house was dead quiet. It was time for me to go. 12:17am, I walked past Mum's door and listened. Everyone was asleep. You could have heard a pin drop, if not for my step-father snoring loud enough to lift the roof off. I turned back around and walked into my room, opened the window and climbed down the old pine tree to the ground. I could not go out the front door because it was locked and I did not have a key.

I walked down the road to the old concert shelter. As I was walking along, I saw an old house. I had seen it before, but somehow it looked different. Maybe it was because it was dark and scary outside, or maybe it happened when the moon came out from behind the clouds and people could see me, but I had what I thought was a bright idea — just go knock on the door, and see if anyone is living there. This was a dumb idea in the end, but I didn't know that yet.

I walked over and knocked on the door. It opened by itself, which was a little creepy, but I was desperate. I called out "Hello, is anybody there?" but got no answer. I walked inside and sat down in the dark room. Soon I fell asleep.

I woke to the sound of my mother talking to someone outside, across the road. I did not know who she was talking to. I did know that I had to get out fast. I slipped out the back door and ran toward the bush. Luckily the moon was out that night, or I would have fallen flat on my face as I dodged engine parts, piles of wood and weeds in the messy yard. I was soon out of breath, but I had managed to make it to the tree line where I could hide.

I walked for quite some time; I'm not sure how long I was out there in the dark. I came across a bunch of old trucks right out in the bush – dump trucks and a few 18 wheelers. I climbed in a container and fell asleep.

Soon enough, the sun started to come up over the hill. I felt like I had just closed my eyes, I was so tired. I knew I would soon run out of food, and sure enough it was all gone by the next morning. I had to go out and look for some on the street. I walked for a half an hour up the road and found myself in front of a corner store. There was milk and bread outside the shop – the 5am deliveries. I took only what I needed – one loaf of bread and one glass bottle of cold milk. I walked back to the truck to sit and think. I had no money, and as the sun went down I knew it would be another long, hungry night.

I walked past that same little corner store every day or two and grab a loaf of bread. I knew it was wrong, but what was I to do? I decided I had to sneak home at some stage and get some more food and a clean set of clothes. I needed a shower badly. I could smell myself, not pretty and very strong on the nose.

A few days later, I had to try it. On my way home, I ran in to my younger brother, riding his BMX bike. He dropped his bike and we hugged. He wanted to know if I was ok, and I told him I was. He promised that he would not tell Mum that he had seen me. We spoke for a bit, and I found out that Mum was not home, so me and my brother walked back to the house together.

I went straight for the shower and was in there for more than ten minutes! I got a clean set of clothes and more food, then hugged my brother again and told him I would be back in a few days. I walked quickly down the street, through the bush and back to the trucks. In the daylight, they looked like they hadn't been driven for a very long time. For the next few days, I ate. I sat and thought about my life and how I could make changes to the way I was living.

After a few more days out there, I was out of food again and starting to stink. I remember my brother saying my mother was not going to be home that day. "This is perfect! Shopping day and she'll be out for hours." If I left straight away, she would be gone and I would be safe. I left the back of the truck and headed up through the bush until I was about a half a street away. I walked around the corner, and there was my mother, waiting for me. My younger brother had told her when I was coming.

"Don't fucking move!" she said, and I froze in fear. Somehow, I could not just walk away like I wanted to, like I should have. Mum came up close, grabbed me by the T-shirt and dragged me all the way home. She told me to sit on the end of the bed and undo the new knots she had done just for me. "I'll deal with you when I get home" was all she said. She left to go shopping, and I knew when she got back I was in for some real trouble.

I write again.

Do you think it is normal to fight with your partner?

Do you think you have the right to punch them in the face?

Why does a young boy have to witness all this violence?

You and he had to hash out your problems, nothing was sorted.

Did you lash out at your child because it made you feel better?

Why did you allow your eldest and your youngest to do whatever they wanted

While I, the middle child, was used as your personal whipping boy?

What did you truly get out of it? Did you not see that I was not that bad?

You fed me, clothed me. This did not give you the right to hurt me!

I'm not a hurtful man at all, but I couldn't care less that you are gone now.

Chapter 6 Close Call

I was thinking of ways I could be a better man while I was undoing those knots. The only plan I could come up with was to go to my mate's place, a few minutes away on my rusty BMX. I arrived to find my mate having a drink. "Do you want one?" "Sure." I answered. "Why not?" We were not going to get wasted on one beer, and I knew I was already in a world of trouble with my Mum anyway.

We drank the beer and talked about my rough few months. "Hey, do you want to go for a walk?" my mate asked. "Yeah, why not?" it was a nice late afternoon - about 6 o'clock. We met another friend who was on his way to see us, just to hang out, and off we all went.

On the other side of the road was a purple Ford Cortina. I've never been into Fords much. "I love my Holden cars" I said, but my friend pointed out that the keys were in the driver's side door and said, "Let's check it out." After much debate and a little bit of fighting, I grabbed the keys and we walked off. One of them suggested we go back when it was dark, and maybe take it for a drive. I was not cool with that idea. "Look," he said, "if we take it we will bring it back, and no-one will know." I said, "I have a bad feeling inside about this."

The three of us waited until it was dark. The whole time, I was trying to convince them that it was all a really bad idea, but they did make a pretty convincing argument about how easy it would be to bring it back before anybody knew it was gone. We walked back to the car, opened the door, put it into neutral and pushed it down the road so that we did not make a sound.

When we thought we had pushed it far enough away, my mate said he wanted to drive it first, and we all agreed and jumped in. He drove it about 20 miles out of town, driving so fast over speed humps that the front of the car bottomed out and came off, and he ran over it. Then it was my turn. I drove back to within a few miles of where we had picked it up. "Hey, it's my turn now!" said my other mate. 'Yes, fair enough, your turn" I answered, "but man! we'd better get it back! We are going to get caught! I will be a dead man if that happens." We changed seats.

Suddenly, he revved the car pretty hard in neutral, then he dropped it straight into drive, doing donuts one after another. Then he made the car slide and skid and almost took out a power pole. After about 15 minutes of doing hand brakes and filling the air with smoking rubber, the car was almost out of fuel and we decided it was time to take it back and leave it where we found it.

We drove up near to where we found it, then turned off the engine and pushed it back to where it had been parked. My mate pulled on the handbrake and put it park. As we walked away, a set of lights appeared behind us, red and blue, and we all turned pale. We knew we just got busted, and I knew I was a dead boy when my mother found out, though I hoped she wouldn't.

The police took the three of us down to the station. We were all questioned about the car. Who took the keys? Who drove it? The police wanted to get to the bottom of the matter, as I expected. As the night wore on, I found out that the other two boys had lied to cover their own arses. They said that I was the one who took the keys, and that I was the only one driving. They claimed that I had bottomed out the car and done all the skids and donuts. I said that this was not true; we all took it and we all drove it.

The officer said, "Sign here." Then I heard the words I never wanted to hear. "We have to call your mother to come and pick you up." I literally almost shit myself as I knew what would come of it. I begged and pleaded, but to no avail. Fifteen minutes later, I saw my mother talking to the officer, who was now giving me the "come here" signal with his fingers. I walked over, ever so slow. As I walked toward my mother I could see my two friends. They were both looking pretty proud of themselves. She thanked the officer for taking care of me and we walked out to the car.

As she unlocked the car door, she said very softly, "I'm going to kill you when we get home. I'm going to tear strips off you." Not a word was spoken the whole trip. I knew what was coming – that damned hose by the arm of the chair. As we pulled up, she said, "Go to bed and we will talk tomorrow". A reprieve? This was not like my mother at all. Maybe she was sick or something, but it was definitely a reprieve and I accepted it without a word. I never slept at all that night.

The next morning at breakfast not a word was spoken about it. I was truly wondering what was going on. Who had taken my mother and replaced her with this imposter? I was not complaining at all! I was just trying to understand. I knew without being told that I was grounded, so I just stayed in my room each day until the case was heard.

On the day of the hearing, the judge gave me a fine to pay for the damages to the car. I had to give an apology to the man who owned the car, which I did. I avoided jail by telling the judge I would no longer hang around with those boys. And after that, I didn't. Jail was not an option I wanted to take. I was lucky and I knew it, so I was going to be a good boy from now on. I would never be so stupid again…or would I?

I write again:

What the hell was I thinking? It was not mine to take! I was an idiot!

Now I'm all grown up

I would be so pissed off if this happened to me

I did apologise to him, to the owner of the car

That was the right thing to do.

I was stupid, but in truth, I did not think 'til after the fact

I can never take back what I did, but I have accepted that's
what I did

I've never broken the law since that stupid-arse day

I never will again.

Chapter 7 Wrong Person

Weeks had passed after the court case, and not a word had been spoken about that night. There was no hose used, and no harsh words. It seemed to me that I had been punished enough, sitting in my room untying a lot of knots she made just for me. One day, I finally finished undoing the knots. It was a fine sunny day outside. I thought for a while about how much I wanted to go for a bike ride to my friend's house, then out I went.

We rode up and down the street for a bit, then I got pulled up by a policeman. He told me to come for a ride with him. I hopped into his white VK Holden Commodore police car – he was a police officer, I had no choice. After a few minutes of driving around, he pulled up outside a red brick house. He asked me if I had seen the house before, and I answered "No, I never go to this end of town. It's out of bounds for me – my mother told me to stay away from here."

The police officer said "Well, someone broke into this house and stole a VCR player." I again said "No." He said "How am I supposed to trust you? You stole a car." He drove me down to the police station for questioning. Once he got me into the interview room, he told the officer already in the room to go and get us some coffee. The other officer nodded to him with a grin and a wink. He knew what was going to happen to me. He left the room and closed the door behind him.

The remaining officer asked me again if I had broken into the house he had taken me to, and I answered "No, sir." He told me "There is another boy here who says you and him broke into that house." My answer was "No, sir, I've already told you I don't go up that way." Boom! No warning; he hit me across the side of my face with a phone book. "I'll ask you again – did you break into that house?" I gave him the same answer "No, sir! I did not go to that house, let alone break in and steal something!" Whack! He hit me on the other side of my head with such force that it spun me out of my chair. I thought "This is not going to stop.'

I got up slowly and went back to my seat. The officer said "I am going to ask you one more time. Did you break into that house?" I said "NO!" and he hit me again, knocking me to the ground. He did not ask again, just said "I will write up a statement and I want you to sign it." I said "OK", still stunned. When he finished, the other officer walked in – no coffee. He brought me the statement and said "Read it, then sign it." I sat there, sore and scared, and read until I came to the part where he had written that I had smashed a window out to break into the house. "No" I said, "I can't sign this, ok, as I did not do it!"

The officer grabbed the phone book again and started to walk toward me. I said "OK! OK! I'll sign it!" I could not stand to be hit like that again. "Where do I sign? I want to go home." "Sign here" he said, "and I'll take you home."

Twenty minutes later, we pulled up outside my house. He walked me to the front door. Knock! Knock! Knock! He bashed it with a commanding air. My mother opened the door. The look on her face was past priceless. The officer said "The boy has been in some trouble. He has a court date soon. Make sure he turns up." She said "Don't worry, Officer. He will be there come hell or high water." The officer walked back to his car, looking daggers at me the whole time he's driving away. My mother put her hand on my shoulder and squeezed it tight. She said quietly "Get the fuck inside."

I went inside, and Mum began ranting and raving and wanting to know what I had done. The look on her face said, "I am going to kill you." After that furious meltdown, she let me speak. I said, "Mum, I never did what he said I did. I know you've told me not to go up that way! Look what he did to me to get me to sign the statement. He kept saying I did it when I did not! I swear on it!" I pulled up my lip. Top and bottom, it was split and bleeding and bruised. She started to rant and rave again. "That policeman dog cunt is going to pay for what he has done to you!"

She took me straight to the police station, and asked to see the chief. She spoke to him in his office, and he told her that there had been a few complaints about the officer in question. He told Mum to make sure to take me to the doctor and get me checked out. "We need to show his injuries in court. I will call in someone here to take photos and write a report." When we left, Mum did take me to the doctor. I had never been "checked out" after head injuries before.

On the day of my court case, I was thinking of taking off because I had heard of what they do to boys in jail. I had only been in trouble a few months before. Would they believe me? My lawyer said, "Don't worry, you're not going to jail." I said, "The judge will likely make his judgement based only on what I did in the past." My lawyer replied, "I have proof that you did not do it." After talking to him, I trusted my gut feeling that it would be ok and went into the waiting room.

I did not have long to wait. The bailiff came out and called my name. I knew it would all be over in a few minutes, one way or the other. I was placed in the dock. The judge asked me "How do you plead?" and I said firmly "Not guilty." The judge told me to be seated.

My lawyer asked for the officer in question to stand in the dock. My lawyer said, "I have one simple question to ask you." The officer said "OK." "Answer this one simple question. It is all I will ask. Answer truthfully; remember you are under oath." He pointed to me and said. "Did you assault this boy?" The officer said, "We are here on the boy's stealing charge." My lawyer simply looked at him, then answered "Yes we are. But my question is a simple one. Just answer it. You are under a solemn oath to tell the truth."

The officer looked glum. The judge said, "Answer the question." The officer said "No."

My lawyer looked at the officer standing there with his hat in his hand. Then he looked at his folder, and said to the judge "May I approach the bench?" The judge said "Yes, you may." He walked up to the bench and the judge leaned over to hear him. When my lawyer finished speaking, the judge nodded. He came back and stood next to me, looked at his folder, and took his time with what came next.

"I will ask you one more time. Remember, you are under oath!" The officer again responded to the question with "No." and said, "I don't see the relevance of what you are asking to this case." Then the lawyer said the words I would never forget. "Get out!" he commanded. The officer just stood there, stunned. The judge nodded at my lawyer, who repeated "Get out!"

The judge said "Officer, it is time for you to leave. Before you do, I would like to inform you that you will be under investigation without pay in this matter; the evidence against you is overwhelming. And I will recommend that if you are ever allowed to work as a police officer again, you will be demoted for at least twelve months. Do as the lawyer said and get out of my courtroom before I charge you with contempt."

The judge looked at me. "I feel justice has been done today. I am sorry that an officer of the law failed you. Case dismissed!"

I will never forget that moment. The officer walked out. I was free to go! I shook my lawyer's hand and praised him for his amazing work on my case. I am sure that without him, I would have gone to jail.

Chapter 8 Turn For The Worse

It seemed like my life might be getting back on track. A month or two passed without drama. I decided to go and have a look at a place I had found where they held concerts in the bush. It was quiet there now; I could sit and put my thoughts together. Not much had changed since the last time I had been there. I looked around, and something caught my eye – the old house where I had once slept.

I went over to take a closer look. It was a very old house. The style made me think it had been built in the early 1900's and clad in weatherboards. Someone had put very old rustic red bricks right over the wood. The old man that owned the derelict house delivered wood for a living. He was always dirty; he looked like he never showered. All he wore was a pair of old football shorts. He was not trustworthy, but I did not know it then.

I wanted to check the house out; it looked so spooky and run down! The lawn had grown about six feet high, and the windows were covered in spider webs. Some were even broken. I walked up to a spot on the fence where three boards were missing, thinking it was a pretty safe bet that no one lived there anymore. I climbed through the hole in the fence, weaving my way through the maze of old tyres, car parts, motors and piles of doors and timber I found under the long grass.

To my shock, there was a lady in the yard, lying on a banana lounge. She saw me, and did not seem at all put out that I was intruding on her private space. She asked me if I wanted to go inside for a smoke - a rather unusual way to react to a complete stranger, I thought. She was very cool under the circumstances. There did not seem to be any harm in it, though, so I went in with her. I had a pack of 15 cigarettes, Peter Jackson, extra mild, dark blue, that I had bought the day before.

We talked for a while and she seemed nice. She had a boyfriend, but he was not there. She told me about her little boy, who was six years old, and invited me to come back for a talk and a smoke. "You are always welcome," she said. "Come anytime, day or night. Maybe you will meet my man next time. Don't bother to knock, just come on through, our house is yours."

They lived like hippies; nothing ever seemed to bother them. They drank and smoked weed, so over the coming weeks I would pop in for a smoke and a cup of tea. It took me some time to get used to not knocking on the badly faded and cracked front door. I remember it was made of thin pine, like a laundry door, painted blue on the inside.

Once when I walked in, she was having sex with her boyfriend and another man. She called out, "We will be out in a minute, just finishing up. Put the jug on and we will have a cup of tea." I did not know which way to look. The image is still stuck in my mind – the boyfriend was doing doggy and the other guy was getting a head job. I did as she asked, put the jug on and while I waited for it to boil, I faced the wall. After a few minutes, she and her boyfriend were sitting at the table, having tea "with milk and one sugar, thanks". The other man walked out and gave her a big bag of weed. "See you again in a couple of weeks," was his farewell comment.

 I did not recognise him then, but I realised that he was a police officer after I saw him in his work clothes. He knew I could bring him down at any time, but what he did not know is that I am not that kind of person. Later, he hunted me down recklessly. It took me a long time to put together that his hatred was based on his fear of what I knew about him. That house was simply my refuge, but he had a bad impression of me because of what went on there. I accepted the norm and didn't think much about.

Heavy drugs, including heroin, were injected daily there. They respected me enough that they did not force me to try it, and I had enough sense to say "No." when it was offered to me. I never did touch hard drugs. What I did like was the whiskey: Southern Comfort and Jack Daniels. I never could work out how they could afford all the drugs and whiskey, always there for whoever needed them.

I was sixteen. I had seen it all, but I was not any wiser for it. One night, I turned up at my younger brother's birthday party drunk. My mother told me to go to bed and sleep it off. When I woke the next day, there was no one in the house. I thought I might as well go down to my friends' house, as usual, and see what they were up to. I walked in without knocking, as I normally did, and saw a new face. Since she was a friend of my friends, I imagined she must be cool. I could not see that she was planning a con; I would never have imagined the part she would play in my life. She seemed to fit right in with the household. That's how the con started.

We talked for a while. She, too, seemed to have had a hard life. She had tattoos! I wanted them so bad, but I was too young. I spent many days over weeks and months, talking and talking, before the moment when my life was turned upside down. Life in that crazy household seemed normal and safe, compared to the life I led with my mother.

On the day of the murder, my mother turned up at the door of the old house. She asked for me, and wanted me to come out. "He's not here," the new lady told her. My mother said "Sorry, I don't believe you. I want my son." "Oh," she said sweetly. "If he comes, I will be sure to send him home to you." I knew my mother knew I was inside; she was not stupid. I left it for a bit, then went home where my mother was waiting. Mum told me she was going to pick up my step-father. "Lay low, he's drunk," was her advice as she went out the door. I was thinking, "What the hell have I done now? I've been good."

An hour later, I heard him yelling in his booming voice. "Where is the little cunt?" You have heard the story of that nightmare fight already, and of my mother's final, deadly response.

 As he choked on his own blood, lying in my arms and swearing he was going to get me, suddenly all I could hear was sirens. Ambulance One. Ambulance Two. Ambulance Three. Four police cars. The street was lit up like Christmas; people came from everywhere. The next-door neighbour was hanging over the fence. Everyone was staring, and I had gone brain dead. It was all a blur and time seemed to be going slow.

Then up walked my favourite police officer. He started asking me questions. I did not even recognise him. He walked me down the driveway to a police car and told me to get in. All I could see was a red and blue blur, and faces looking in at the window. I saw my little brother run up the driveway, then I went blank.

The next thing I can remember is being in a room with detectives, who were asking me all kinds of questions. The interrogation went on for hours. At 3:30am I was asked to come into another room where my brothers were waiting. Once I was there, we were given the news that my step-father had passed away during surgery. My little brother had lost his father.

That night, we stayed with relatives. The next day, the family was broken up. Some woman came and took my little brother away. My older brother rented a room at the pub, and I ended up walking the street all night and watching the sun rise. The only place I could think of to go was back to my house, where I stayed for a little over a week. There was food in the fridge and in the pantry. After a few days, the power was shut off.

On the third day, the step-father's brother's wife turned up with a big removal truck. She had come to take everything, although all he owned was a small table and a book case. "Pretty big truck for that," I said. I told her she could take those two items, but nothing else. "No, sorry, little boy, I'm here to take it all." I said firmly, "You had better take off before the police are called." She took my sound advice and left.

On the seventh day, my older brother came and took everything out of the house, on Mum's instructions. I had no power, no food and no clothes. All I had left in the world were the friends in that old house who had kept me sane. So I went there, thinking I had no other choice.

It was a mistake.

Chapter 9 Only The Begining

I went to the old house. I could hardly read the number, eighty-nine, on the old, rusty mailbox sitting on bluestone rocks on the ground. The rocks continued as a path to the door. I walked in; nobody home. I knew I was welcome, day or night.

I was there for three days before anyone else arrived home. The second lady came in; the one who had been so nice to me. She said that I was more than welcome to stay. I told her I did not know how long I would be staying – life was a bit all over the place. And I thanked her.

It was good to be grounded, and away from my mother, but was life finally going to be what it was cracked up to be? I knew only time would tell. I chopped wood for the stove and fire place to help pay my way. The first woman I met and her boyfriend got kicked out the same day for not paying the rent. She spoke to the old woodman, the landlord, and arranged for us to stay.

He was a crazy old man. He once burned down a house that had been handed down to him after his father's death. He stood up on the hill and watched it burn, I have been told. He did not call for emergency services to come and put it out until it was well alight and beyond saving. It was a big old farm house with pig pens and chook runs, a beauty. No one could ever prove he did it, but I knew he was crazy enough for sure! He said we could stay, as long as we paid the rent. She agreed to his terms and it was done.

When she took over the place she made me feel welcome. She said she wanted to help, because of all I had been through. But there was no trick she did not know how play. It took me years to find out about everything she had done, but she slowly got inside my mind, creating confusion and doubt.

My first experience of her cunning – and stupidity – was a story she made up about the people who had just moved out. She said that they had run up a $450 bill on my account at the shops for food and smokes. There certainly was a bill for $450 – I found that out when I went to the shop the next day to sort the mess out. It was only a two-minute walk away.

As I walked up, I saw a police car out the front of the shop. I thought nothing of it as I went to the counter to talk with the owner of the shop. Tap, tap, I felt a hand on my shoulder. The police officer asked, "Where were you last night?" "At home, sir" I replied. "Why are you asking?" He told me the front window of the shop had been smashed in with a Southern Comfort bottle filled with urine. I suddenly thought of the woman I lived with.

I spoke to the owner, explaining that I had not given anyone permission to use my account. I asked him who had done it. "It was that woman up the road you are sharing the house with, the blonde lady" he said. "Seeing you had no clue what she was doing, we will just add it to her account and you can pay your normal amount." I paid my bill, then left swiftly to go talk to the lady herself.

When I got in, I asked her why she had thrown a bottle of piss through the window of the shop. She said, "I never did! But I would shake the hand of the person who did it! He deserves every little bit he gets." I was shocked. I asked her why she put $450 worth of smokes and food onto my account. Once again she said "It was not me! It was the other two who lived here!" I told her that the shop owner had said it was her. She had her cover ready. "The other lady dyed her hair blonde that day! Can't you see it wasn't me?"

I just had to put it aside. It was doing my head in. I had not seen the other lady for some time. She might be right...but I knew it was her. I could not prove it yet. I went to bed early, and when I woke up early the next day she was already gone.

I decided to go for a walk and saw some of my old school friends on the street. They pointed at me, then looked at each other, turned away, and walked off. It was strange and a bit rude, but I thought nothing of it until it happened again. I saw a girl I liked from school, and she did the same. She looked right at me. I waved. Then she put her head down and walked away like I wasn't even there.

I was beginning to get it. Maybe I was being judged, like I was at school. My mother could not afford proper school clothes for me, so she dressed me in whatever she could find at the second-hand store. One time, the only pants that would fit me were lime green, with flares. The shoes she bought were black, at least, but looked like a cross between clown shoes and witches' shoes, due to a very large silver buckle across the front. At first, I kept a set of old school clothes in my bag, so I wouldn't have to wear the "new" clothes. But that didn't last – my older brother told my mother what I had in my bag and my old clothes disappeared. I became a laughingstock, to say the least. Everybody pointed at me and stared and laughed. That's what it felt like – but the difference was that nobody was laughing.

I knew something was up, so I decided to go back to the house. I had not long walked in the door when I heard a knock. It was a welfare officer, checking on me, a minor, 16 years old. She was making sure I was fed and clothed. I told her I was fine; I was being well looked after. She took some notes and left within five minutes of arriving.

I was in the kitchen making a cup of tea when bang! Smash! A bike helmet came flying through the kitchen window. I froze. What the hell was going on here? The "lady" of the house came roaring in, accusing me of sleeping with the welfare officer! I said "She was just here to check on me. There was no sleeping together! You and I are not dating, we're just friends, so what does it have to do with you anyway?" She said she did not trust men, and she was just trying to help me by putting a roof over my head.

I still did not understand what her rage was about. I was so tired. I had no fight left in me to stick up for myself, and I had grown to hate drama. What I did know was that this woman had taken me in when everyone else was shunning me. I was being judged because of what my mother had done. I still had her court case ahead of me, and she was still in jail. All sorts of stories were going around. But I had a roof over my head. It could have been so much worse for me. Anyway, I was used to being all alone in the world. She finally stopped going on about it and I went to bed.

When I woke, I found my favourite jeans missing. My watch - I had found it in the dirt, but it worked a treat! Was also gone, as was my best T-shirt, black with a white Motörhead logo on it. I turned the house upside down looking for them. She said she had not seen them; I knew different but could not prove it. I could not find them anywhere. It was a strange feeling. I knew the watch was in the front pocket of my jeans and that the jeans and T-shirt had been right beside my bed where I had undressed a few short hours before. I thought to myself "I'm not stupid, but I don't have the strength in me left to fight".

 Stranger things began to happen from this time on. Before I had time to organise my life, we were getting kicked out. She had not been paying the rent, which I then found out was only $50 a week. I also found out that she had been taking the rent from the other two tenants and not passing it on to the landlord. We were forced to move into a caravan at a caravan park, which was ok, but only lasted a month or so. We got a new place, a flat on top of an old shoe store in town. The owner of the shop was our landlord; a very nice man. Like many others, he put up with a lot of nonsense from her. She could con the devil and she was very good at lying.

Chapter 10 Still After Me

After we were there for a few weeks, I could hear the front door handle rattling, like someone was trying to get in. I walked up to the door and looked through the eye piece. What a shock! It was the policeman who had bashed me at the station. He was on his own. He was trying all the windows, trying to get in. Why? Nothing clicked right away, and after a few more minutes, he was gone. I was trying to put all the pieces together when I remembered. He was the third guy in the threesome I had walked in on at that strange old house, number eighty-nine.

"Why would he want to hassle me?" I asked myself. It did not make sense. Too much was going on in my mind, but all would be resolved in time. That night, the woman I lived with asked me if I wanted to go out to dinner to her son's house. He had invited us both. I thought, "Why not?" It was a nice night and his house was only fifteen minutes away walking, so off we went.

As we were walking, I could hear a car following slowly behind us. I turned to look. It was that police officer again in that same white VK Holden Commodore. Once we got to her son's house, I could see him just sitting in his car down the road, watching and waiting – for what? Her son thought that he was following me because of what I knew about him. He was married and had children, but I knew that he was sleeping around and taking drugs, and to top it off I knew he was a boy in blue and I could get him in a lot of trouble. "Yes," I thought to myself. "That makes perfect sense."

We sat down to dinner; T-bone steak with chips and vegetables and mushroom gravy. The meal was lovely, but I was still thinking of how I could get this officer off my back. I was cleared of the false charges that he put on me. The whole story was beginning to fall into place…

We finished our dinner and said our goodbyes. He was still sitting there in his police car when we walked out the door, engine started, headlights on. The car began to follow us slowly up the road. Just up the road was a pay phone. I decided to call the police station and explained to the officer's superior what was going on. He said, "Just give me five minutes."

I could hear the officer being told through his radio to move on. He said, "I am following a known criminal." His superior said "I am not asking you, I am ordering you! Now move on!" The car moved past me slowly, and he was looking at me as if to say, "You won this round", but I am happy to say that I never did hear from that officer again.

Once we got home, I went straight to bed, my refuge. When I woke up, she was giving herself a Tarot reading. I said, "What is this crazy shit people believe in?" She said she had just finished doing her reading and could do one for me. I thought, "Why not? There's no harm in it – it's just a deck of cards." She began to lay down the cards, telling me the story behind each one as she placed it on the table. The first card told her that I would be looked after by a blonde-haired lady. The second card said that I have been through a very hard life and everything will be ok. Card number three was about changes coming to do with moving, and the fourth card spoke of me as a strong spirit who needed to believe in himself a bit more. The fifth, and final card was a bit more disturbing. "You will lose everyone that you are close to within the next six months."

I was thinking that it was all rather strange when I heard a knock on the door. It was a summons to go to court as a witness in my mother's murder trial. Then I got a call from the prosecutor, asking me to come see him to discuss my mother's case. I said, "Sure, I'll come straight down." He asked me a lot of questions. What was my mother like as a mother? What was she like as a partner to my step-father? I told him the truth. I did not know that he was not supposed to speak to me. I found that out when my mother's lawyer contacted me to tell me how the case was going.

Another month passed. It was time to go to court for her bail hearing. I had not seen my brothers for almost two months. Bail was granted and the final hearing date to hear the case was set. She was free for three months.

I went to see her at the friend's place. I thought it was the right thing to do. She and her friend were sitting in the dining room, having tea and cake. My mother said "I can't wait for this to be over! Then you will be coming home to live with me." I said, "Mum, I am out of home now. I have been for months. I won't be coming back home." With that, she slapped me so hard across my face that the blow perforated my eardrum. "You will do as you are told! And you will be coming home!" I left then and there, with my mother screaming the whole time. That was the last I'd see of her till the day of the court case.

I write again.

You tried to bring me down

You made up lies, you tried to sell me out

I was not smart enough to see it right away

I did not care about what you did, it was not my place

You clearly were worried, you were married with children as well

How did I not see? I was confused by your actions towards me

You played one too many games, and it backfired

Now who is stupid?

Chapter 11 Twisted

Months passed, and the lease came up again. My evil landlady told the owner she wanted to move, which just happened to work out well for her son. He was leaving the place he was in and said that we could take over the lease. One condition – he would keep a room there and use it whenever he needed it. I thought, "Oh well, not a bad idea. At least it is a house with a yard." I agreed to the new arrangement. That settled, she told me we were out of smokes and bread and sent me off to the shops to get some.

Years later, I discovered that she knew that my uncles were planning to come to visit me that day. Off I went, not knowing her motive was to prevent me from knowing I had a choice of who to stay with. They had come to offer me a place to live, with family who cared about me. No sooner had my uncles arrived and knocked on the door, she was out the front telling them "Fuck off! He does not need or want you in his life!" And of course, they left, and left me alone as they thought I had requested.

Years later, we had a massive fight when I found out what she had done. She would not admit it and continued to claim that my whole family had left me for dead when my mother went to jail. On the surface, that seemed to be true. I did not find out the whole truth until I was an adult. She knew how to manipulate me, combining truth and lies and twisting them together to get her own way. I was just a boy and she knew I wanted more than anything to feel safe. She gave me that sense of security with a great big dish of crazy on the side. It was only two days until my mother's court case, so she behaved herself until after the case was finished.

The day of the case itself was crazy and overwhelming for me. My mother's lawyer showed me where to sit and told me what to do and where to go when my name was called. It did not sound too hard, but little did I know at that moment what was about to go down. The prosecutor's case was strongly based on my testimony.

Once everyone was seated, her lawyer gave a rundown of that frightful night. Many witnesses answered questions from both the lawyer and the prosecutor. After hearing many witnesses, my name was called. I put my hands on the Bible and swore to tell the truth, the whole truth and nothing but the truth. First, my mother's lawyer asked the questions. Then the prosecutor started, and I realised that what I said would put the final nail in the coffin of my mother's defense. The truth would set me free from the years of abuse, but it would condemn my mother.

The prosecutor fired his questions at me from every direction. Then he began to speak about what I had told him the day we went into his office. He could see my mother sitting in the dock wondering what I was going to say. He asked me "Did your mother ever hit you?" I answered "Yes." "Has she ever hit you with a piece of garden hose? Before you answer, please that a minute to gather your thoughts. Give the court a full account of these incidents. Remember that you have sworn to tell us the truth, and all the truth."

I looked at my mother. I could see in her eyes that she knew that her dreams of getting out of jail were about to be crushed. I gave a full account of each incident I could remember. The he asked, "Did you witness the stabbing of the deceased by the defendant yourself?" I said "Yes. Sir. I saw my mother stab my stepfather." The prosecutor told me to stand down and go back to my seat.

The case went on a few more days, hearing the testimony of many witnesses. Finally, the last day came. The jury brought in their decision. "Do you find the defendant guilty or not guilty of murder?" "Not guilty", came the response. "Do you find the defendant guilty or not guilty of manslaughter?" "Guilty" was the verdict. The court went silent. I looked around. I could not believe what I had just heard.

My mother was taken away to await sentencing. The judge went in to deliberate on all he had heard and decide on a just punishment. We all just waited. I was in shock.

The judge returned with his decision. He sentenced her to four and one-half years in prison. I thought to myself, "Where is the crime? Yes, my mother treated me very badly, but what about his treatment of her? And what about his violence against me and her need to protect me?" But the judge's decision was final, and I was not about to question that. Mum was led away to serve her sentence.

That night, I got drunk and cried like a baby for my mother. I was uncertain about my future – even though my mother was a rough nut, life with her was the only life I really knew. I was lost. I felt ashamed for not stopping my step-father that night. I felt like I had lost part of my soul for not being a man and standing up against his bullying.

It took me many years to realise that if a terrorised sixteen-year-old boy freezes and doesn't "stand up" to a drunken, murderously violent adult male, it is not a reflection on his "manhood"! I was only a boy and I had many lessons to learn. I spent a long time after that learning the hard way and learning fast. My character was tested far beyond what I ever thought I could handle, often in ways that made me question my sanity as well as my manhood.

Here is an example. On the way home after the court case, the woman I shared a house with said "I think it would be a great idea if we went up to the old house tonight. I have a gut feeling about it. I did a card reading last night and it told me so." I just said I was in no mood for stupid games after the gut-wrenching finish of the case. She began to swear and carry on, yelling "You don't really get it! We really need to go to that house tonight because there is something following you! We need to go to the old house and find out what it is!" I gave in and said "Ok, fair enough." All the drama was beginning to do my head in.

We waited until it got dark and headed up to the old place. It was as empty as the day we moved out; nothing had changed. All of a sudden, she called out from the kitchen "You need to see this!" There were my favourite jeans and shirt, the ones which had disappeared, all ironed and laid out on the floor as if someone was wearing them. "This is freaky, to say the least," I thought. "But where is the watch?" Strange things seemed to be starting to happen.

We left and got back home late. When we walked in the door, we discovered her son had moved back in, which didn't bother me at all. He had a nice fire going in the fire place in his room and had left the door open, warming the whole house. Everything was normal. I said goodnight to them both and went to bed.

Over the next week, he often had a fire going. He decided to clean out the ash when the fireplace was cold. He found something in the ashes and called his mother to have a look. She inspected his find and told me to have a look. It was my watch, that had gone missing over a year before. There was not a scratch on it; it had not melted or blown up in the blazing fire. "This is strange," I thought, really puzzled.

But later that day I realised that it was all just too much of a coincidence – her asking to go to the old house and finding the clothes; the watch turning up in the fire. She had taken the clothes and watch, and she had put them out in those weird places so we could "find" them. She never admitted it. How could she? It would make her look like she did crazy shit for sure. And she did.

She started an account in a little shop just ten minutes away from our house. She told me that they let her have the account because she knew their family well. I never thought about it again until one day a few months later. We both walked into the shop at the same time. The lady behind the counter said hello to her, then hello to me, but called me by a name that was not my own. I was about to correct her, but my housemate jumped in and said, "This is my son Chris, and yes, I give him permission to get whatever he needs." I thought "What the hell…?!" I could not get a word in until we left a few minutes later. As we walked out of the shop the owner said "Bye, Chris". I just said my goodbyes really fast and walked out.

I was ready to have a go at her for more lies and more games. She said she had to say I was her son because they only give accounts to families. I said, "But you told me you knew their family." "Well!" she huffed. "I never said such a thing!" "Wait a minute!" I protested. "Are you trying to drive me barmy?" She would never admit her lies.

She never told me any of her secrets, and before you knew it there was a new lie, a new scam. She would fight tooth and nail to keep them going, and say she was protecting me. On one of these frustrating days, I asked her how this behaviour was protecting me. The only answer I got was "Why are you questioning my motives and character?"

At this point, I had not seen my younger brother since the night it all went to hell. I had only seen my older brother a few times. Whenever I tried to approach him, she would start to threaten him and tell him that she would get her biker friends to bash him up if he did not leave me alone. Finally, I thought "Stuff this" and told her I was leaving when we got home. I went in and started to pack. I didn't have much, so it didn't take long.

As I was going out the front door, she went psycho, screaming and yelling at me wildly. "You would have nothing if it wasn't for me! You would not have had a place to stay!" That much was true. Something held me back, and she continued, "Where are you going? Who is going to take you in? You have seen how people look at you and judge you. Stop being silly and come back inside." What possessed me to turn around and walk back inside? I still don't know. Maybe it was fear of the unknown that kept me there so long.

Chapter 12 Games

A few years passed. My mother was released; she had been a model inmate. I was happy for her, but I was not going home. She was just as nasty, or even meaner, than the horrible woman I already lived with. When she got out, it took me a while to decide to go and see her. During that time, my older brother had been seeing our father. That was his business; I wanted nothing to do with him. From what my mother had told me, he was as bad as my stepfather.

When I went to see my mother, she made me dinner because it was my birthday. I thought that would be as good a time to see the whole family as any. I arrived at Mum's place and she gave me a hug. She thanked my house mate for taking care of me. My housemate told her it was her pleasure, as I was such a "good boy". "Boy? WTF?" I thought as we all walked inside.

When we got inside, my mother said "Before I give you your birthday present, I want to show you what I got for your brothers when I got out of jail. I got them each a "welcome home" present. I got your older brother a gold chain, and the younger boy got a barbell set." I said "Wow, Mum! Those are awesome gifts!" I wondered what I got as a present, as she passed the package to me. I could feel it was soft, and not very heavy, but I opened it with gusto. It was a jumper. I was lost for words. "I didn't have a lot of money left after getting things for your brothers" she commented casually. I asked where she got it. "From the second-hand store" she said. "Oh…Ok" was all I could say. Then the phone rang, and my mother said she would be right back.

I half followed her, then nipped into my older brother's room to see if he had anything of mine. When my mum went to jail, all of my stuff was put away somewhere. While I was looking around, I found my belt buckle. It was a rare Harley Davidson piece that had a link chain around it. I knew it was mine because of the big scratch on the back of it. But this was not an item that had been taken away when Mum went to prison. This had been taken from the house that I shared with my flatmate! I thought to myself "I wonder how he got hold of it?" and put it in my pocket where no one could see it.

I then found a Playboy magazine in his drawer and thought "I'll open it to the Centrefold and lay it under his sheets for Mum to find. Payback!" Payback for the time when I was a very little boy and he put a present, nicely wrapped up, in my bed. I found it there, and I was so excited! It was hard and didn't rattle, but I couldn't wait to open it. Inside? A spud.

Payback completed, I started to walk back to the family. I overheard my mother saying "Yes, yes, I'll keep him here. Don't be too long, I don't know how long I can make him stay." She hung up the phone and walked back into the other room. I came in too and said "Anyways, Mother, I'm going now." She said "No! You can't go yet! You have to have your cake. Your father made it for you! It's a cherry cake." I told her "Mom, I hate cherries. I'm going now." "Don't be a selfish little git" was her response, so I grabbed my jumper and got in the car. I was a 1964 EH Holden wagon, mustard coloured. I belonged to a friend of mine. We got out of there with moments to spare.

When I got home, I called my mum and had a go at her for trying to sneak my father in on me when I did not want to meet him – at least, not like that, thrusted upon me without my consent. My mother said, "Well, son, you don't have a choice. We are getting married again and we both want you to be a part of the wedding." I said I might need some time to think about it. She replied "Ok, but one last thing before you hang up. If you don't meet your father, you are no longer part of this family." Then she hung up on me.

I was lost for words again. What had I done wrong? Why would she go back to him? She had told me what he did to her. He was just like my step-father. How could she? Playing around with other women; beating on her; gambling his wages away; walking out on the family the day I was born were just some of his sins. This made no sense to me, but I did know I would never go to their wedding.

The wedding never happened anyway. He walked out on her 12 months later. And I will add that it had nothing to do with me! Mum finally realised that he had not changed. The lady I lived with was right in the thick of it, keeping my hatred of my father very alive, reminding me frequently that he had abandoned me and my mother and never had tried to see me. She defended my mother, even though she did not get on with her.

She did not stop her crazy games to try to keep me grounded, stuck wherever she was. When a week or two had passed, it was time to go into town to get food for the fortnight. On the way to town, I ran into my younger brother and it did not end well. He abused me and blamed me for the death of his father. He said he would never forgive me. He had many grievances about how Mum and I couldn't get on and how his childhood was stolen from him by his father's death. He needed someone to blame so I took the blows to my chest and listened to abusive language he dished out. I knew he was grieving and I still felt guilty about not stepping in to stop the two of them before the fight became lethal. If I had stepped in, I do not know where it would all have ended. I felt it was ok for my brother to say the things he did; to this very day I feel guilt and shame that I did not try to stop the fight. He left in a huff.

When he left, I stood there battered and broken inside. She told me I had no one in the world on my side but her. And, for a while, I believed her. After she talked to me like that, we went shopping. I told her I just did not want to talk about it anymore. It was doing my head in.

I write again

It was a confusing time for me

In years, I was a man now

I knew she was just as bad as my flat mate

I was stuck in between a rock and a hard place.

I had already lived sixteen years under one ruthless bitch

Time would show who was the worst of them all.

I disliked my mother, and my flatmate I disliked as well

My step-father was dead…

Oh, well

He was a nasty man.

Chapter 13 Sister

My mother sent me a letter asking me to explain to her why my younger brother was so upset. He had gone home that day and told her what we had spoken about. One sentence stood out. "If you don't come home and get away from that evil woman you share a house with, I will have to wipe you as my son." I did not yet understand that the two women were each as bad as the other. My housemate read the letter and hit the roof. "See! I told you what your whole family is trying to do to you!" The big fight was on; back and forth about who trusted who.

I never won a fight with her. She was a nut job who turned everything around and never, never backed down. She was 20 years older than me too. But that never stopped me from trying to get to the bottom of every fight, to try to understand what was impossible to understand in her twisted arguments.

Around this time, I found out in a letter from my older brother that I have a sister. There was a photo of her attached. She was so innocent; she knew nothing of what my life had been like. When she was told that she had another brother, of course she wanted to meet me. But we did not meet for a long time. I cannot justify not meeting her then. I had reasons, but they are not excuses. Later, I was so lucky that when I went looking for her she gave me a chance to talk with her. Now, we talk all the time!

When my housemate found out I had a sister, instead of being happy for me, she went nuts, saying "Look, it's your mother saying this! She is trying to get to your heart because she knows you have always wanted a sister. Now all of a sudden, Bam! You've got one. Your family are clutching at straws to try to get you back. They know you are happy here, and they hate it." And so we fought some more. I told her I was not happy with her, but I would not be happy with my mother either. They were too much alike.

With that, she picked up a heavy glass ashtray and threw it at me. She went absolutely berserk, as she had so many times before. Maybe she did not like my observation about her similarity with my mother. I tried to leave again, but she was not having it. The only way I could get some peace was to say I was sorry and wait for the storm to pass. And from that moment on, my home became a prison, although I did not see it at first.

The very next day, we went to the hardware store to get some screws and two deadlocks for the front and back doors of the house. When we got home, she put in place the first phase of her well-oiled plan. "You go do the front and back doors" she said. "Put the new locks in good and proper. Once you've done that, come and see me. We had prowlers around last night and I don't want no one to get in."

I did not see what was coming. Without haste, I took my toolbox and fitted the locks front and back. While I was busy doing that, she grabbed my drill and drilled holes in all the windows and screwed them shut – even in the loo!

When I finished, I went to find her. She was in the kitchen, making a cup of tea. She asked me politely to go get the keys and put them on the table. I still did not catch on to what was about to happen. I went and got the keys for the two doors and put them on the table as she had asked. Then she said "Could you please do me one more favour? Go under my bed and grab the metal box from under the bed. You'll see it; it's the only thing under there." I went to her bedroom and looked under the bed. There it was - a black metal box. It had hand painted flowers on the lid, white and yellow and red. I picked it up; it was heavy for its size and very solid.

I took the box to the table and set it down in front of her. She asked for my keys. I took them out of my pocket and gave them to her. She took them and put the two new keys on the ring – one for the front, one for the back. Then she put the other two keys on her key ring. As she was putting on the last key, she asked me to go get my bank book. I could not get money out of the bank without it back then. She also wanted my wallet and licence. "Why do you want them?" I asked, still not seeing what she was planning. "Hurry up!" she commanded. "Just grab them! Hurry up!" And I did.

I came back with all she had asked for. She snatched the keys, bank book, driver's licence and wallet, stuck them in the box and put the lock on it. She passed the box back to me. "Put that back where you got it from," she commanded. "Why did you put my things in that box?" I asked.

She answered very clearly. "I don't trust you. I know that between your mother, your brothers and now your sister, who was about six when she left, I know that they will turn you against me. Look at everything I've done for you! I protected you when your mother was in jail! Look at who fed you and clothed you!" All I could think was, "Are you for real?"

Unfortunately, she was dead serious. No matter what she believed, what she was doing was absolutely wrong. She had no right to hold me against my will. I dropped the box to the floor and fell in a heap, sobbing and crying like a little boy.

She made sure that every time we left the house, she had her keys. Everything of mine was in the black box, just where she wanted it to be. Even though the front and back doors were deadlocked when she went out, she checked them two or three times just to be sure. Clearly she did not trust me, and this did not make the situation any easier to swallow. I was not a dishonest person by nature, but I began to make little plans to reclaim my freedom. She was always two steps ahead of me.

One day, her son called to say his car had broken down. He asked if I could come to help him. She was going to see a friend, but she knew that she was safe because she had my bank book and wallet, and I could not get far without them. She dropped me off and drove away.

We started fixing the car. It was just the starter motor, a simple fix. I tried to tell him what his mother was doing to me, but he would not have a bar of it. No help there. I knew I could not just up and leave and go back to my mother. That was never an option, not when I thought of all I had gone through at her hands in the past. For now, I was stuck.

One day, when the son was living with us, he bought a new motor bike. He wanted to show it off, so he took it up the steep hill past the roundabout where I could not see him but could still hear the roar of the bike. As he came down, he jumped the intersection and landed it coming down the hill. He pulled up out the front of the house and yelled "Woohoo! I'm doing it again!" Back up the hill, he jumped the intersection like he was a stunt man, and soon someone called the police.

They began chasing him round and round the block, and each time around he got further ahead. Then there was quiet for a few minutes, and we thought that he had either been caught or was gone because they couldn't catch him. We went inside, excitement over.

A few minutes later, I heard the bike at the front door. He was screaming "Let me fucking in!" As I ran to the door, I could hear the motor rev right up. He dropped the clutch and headed for the door. Bang! He took the door off its hinges, flew in and parked the bike perfectly in the hallway, all in one smooth motion and with only millimetres to spare on either side of the handlebars. I gave him a hand lifting the door back up. It was on a bit of an angle, but we got it up just seconds before the police came roaring past.

The son was laughing. "What a fucking rush!" was all he could say.

Another time, that same son made some hash cookies and tried to get me to eat them. I said, "Nah, I'm good. I know what is in them!" Then another one of her sons turned up and saw the cookies. "I'm starving! Can I have some?" I said nothing. His brother said, "Yes, I just made them, have as many as you like." Well, he ate the whole lot! After about ten minutes, he said, "I'm going for a ride on my new road trail bike." I said to him "Are you sure?" "I'm fine," he said, and out the front he went.

What did he do? He started it, then just sat on it, smiling. I looked at the bike. There was a portrait of Daffy Duck on the front of it where you have a number if it's a racing bike. He kept revving the bike, saying "I feel strange." "Well," I said, "Turn it off." He told me it did not have an off switch, just a wire you had to touch on the handlebars to make it stop.

All of a sudden, the throttle got stuck on full revs. "All I can do is dump the clutch!" he screamed out, "That should stop it! At the count of three I'll drop it! Three! Two! One!" Bam! It bounced five feet in the air and he managed to let it go. He hit the ground laughing as he watched his bike spinning in the road. He found it so funny! The fellow next door was hanging over his balcony, laughing his head off. He kept saying "Daffy Duck in full flight!" which made them laugh even more.

There is another memory that sticks out when I think of her sons. Many years later, the son who ate the cookies had a white WB Holden van. He had just left my place when it broke down. He tried to start it; no luck. I offered to look at it. Soon I was under the bonnet, but without the right tools it was hard to figure out what was going wrong. Her son lost his temper and yelled "If I had a hammer, I would smash this piece of shit!" I tried to cool him down, but no luck. So I thought, "Well, I'll join in." I said, "Well, fuck, I'll grab a hammer and I'll fix it for you!"

Then he had to change his mood and try quiet me down! I said, "No, you don't get to come to my home and tell me to quiet down. No, stuff it. It is my place, not yours. Don't tell me to be quiet when you are going crazy in my street!" I got the van going in the end and he left.

What a day that was! I finally stood up for myself.

Chapter 14 Axe

The years just rolled on past. It did not feel like ten years since my mother had gone to jail. I had lost all hope of breaking free – she had confused and terrified me so often that I had no fight left. I was a man now, but still a boy in so many ways, trying to get through life and make sense of all the things that just didn't make sense.

I remember one day when she was picking on me. Her abusive talk was the norm, but this time I had a great plan. I would just walk off and close the lounge room door behind me so I couldn't hear her. I walked off, ignoring her shouting, went out and gently closed the door. All was strangely silent – for less than a minute. Then I heard an almighty bang, and I'll bet you any money you can't guess what was happening. She was smashing the door down with an axe! I ran and hid behind a big old chair that sat in the corner of the room.

Within two minutes she had totally smashed her way through the door. It was such a beautiful old door, solid pine with a nice grain running through it. I can see it now. She was screaming "I'm going to smash you in the face with this axe when I get hold of you! Just wait till I get in there!" Once the door was shattered into a thousand pieces, she found me behind the chair.

I was quivering with fear, looking up at a lady standing over me with an axe and wondering what was going to happen next. Then suddenly the look in her eyes changed. A second before, she had been a totally crazy person. Now she looked almost sorry for what she had done. She put out her hand and pulled me out from my hiding place.

"Why did you slam the door in my face and lock it?" she demanded. I said, "I did not slam the door. And the door has no lock on it. If you think that I did that, I am sorry. But I didn't." She told me that she hated it when doors were closed on her; that it really set her off.

Later, in the evening, her son came home and asked her what had happened to the door. "We had a fight and he locked me out so I smashed down the door," she answered. "The door has no lock!" I protested. "Well…then you put something up against it to stop me from coming in", she argued. In reality, the door opened outward toward her, so even if I had put something up against it she could still have come in.

I decided that since the day had been hard enough already, I would just keep my mouth shut. And I did. I went into the lounge room and started a fire in the fireplace, using pieces of the smashed-up door. I had just gotten the fire going when I began to daydream, remembering past fights. There was not one time that her rage was justified.

I never saw her outbursts coming. A new place had opened for lunch in town. T-bone steak and chips! As sat with my landlady, ready to eat up, in walked a young woman. She asked me if I had a light, as the gas in her lighter had just run out. "Fuck off, you dog slut!" rang through the restaurant before I could reply. The woman said "Sorry, I was only after a light, that's all." I reached across and lit her cigarette for her. "I'm so sorry for this" I said. She smiled at me softly and walked off. But while I was lighting the cigarette and as she walked away, my companion was mouthing off, calling her all the dogs and all the sluts under the sun. Then she ran out the door.

When she came back in, she looked at me and said "What the fuck was that all about? I seen the way she looked at you." Inside, I was going "What the fuck?!?" but couldn't get a word in as she went on "Did you see how tight her jeans were? Do you know her?" I said "No. I have never seen her before." "What about how she just walked up to you? I bet she wanted to fuck you!" I replied "Who knows if she did? That would be okay. I am single!" "Did you see she asked you for a light and not me?" she continued. "This is crazy talk!" I said, fed up. That was not a smart thing to say to her. I found out later that she had done a stint in the nut house, and she took my comment right out of context.

She looked at me and her eyes glazed over with that crazy look a dog gets before it attacks. "I was watching her!" she said. "We are getting out of here right now!" We walked out, and she stormed right past the bus stop. I was thinking "What the hell is she doing?" so I just followed her. It was over an hour's walk home, and she harangued me the whole time. "Did you see that blonde-haired slut? I know her game! Skin tight jeans, tits hanging all over the place and her makeup made her look like a prostitute, a lady of the night. I know she wants to take you away from me!"

I said, "But we are not together." "Don't be a smart ass!" she retorted. "You know what I mean! I've kept you safe, warm, fed and clothed." I reassured her that I knew and appreciated that she had looked after me. But still she raged on, getting out the anger before we got home. Her moods were extreme and could change in a split second. I was not surprised when I learned that she had been given shock treatment - her unpredictable mood swings were dangerous.

When we got home, she went to prepare a meal. We had left before I could touch my food. I went and got the fire going. Now, in my imagination, I am sitting by that fire, wondering about what had happened…and I then I come out of my daydream and I am sitting by the fire, but now it has gone out. I got a good fire going again and sat down to think about a past I was trying to escape. But that past was my present as well.

So I write again:

You chased me with an axe. I believe you would have killed me.

You know the god damn truth. Stop lying to everyone.

The door had no lock on it. You know the truth, don't you?

You never cared for anyone else's things or feelings, only your own.

You lied and cheated your way through life even to your children –

I hear you say one thing to me and something different to them.

You ran up bills and moved just so you would not have to pay

Everyone you came in contact with, you deceived.

I caught you out in hundreds of lies and scams

There is no decency in you, no moral code.

At least I won't believe another thing that comes out of your mouth.

Chapter 15 Wrong Name

Stalemate. My life was stopped before it started. When I tried to make a move, she was always there: checkmate. Controlling other people was just a game to her. She loved to play it, to have someone's life in her hands. I could see how she revelled in the feeling of raw power when she got her way through manipulation or bullying.

One sunny day, we walked up to the corner store together. I saw a lady leave the shop as we walked in. I had seen her before. She always wore the same clothes – a big mesh garden hat, large sunglasses, a creamy long-sleeved top and dark long pants. She walked with a stick and had a limp. We took no real notice of her and went about the business of getting bread and milk. What we did not see was that she had doubled back after she left and was waiting for us. We paid for our goods and walked out.

We met her face-to-face. She pointed her stick at me. Her first words to me were, "Don't you remember me?" Confused, I said "Sorry, lady, I don't know you at all." She pulled down her glasses. "What the fuck!" I thought. "It's my mother!" I had not spoken to her in ten years. We hugged. She whispered, "Son, I've never stopped loving you." She gave me her number, saying, "You most likely will not call me."

Well! Guess who started? "Why would he want to call you, black coon cunt?" Then it was on for young and old! It was not the first battle between these old warhorses, but neither realised this time would be the last. "Who are you calling a black coon cunt? You are nothing but a used-up nut-job who needs a lifetime of therapy!" "At least I did not bash my son within an inch of his life!" "The fact is, you slept with all the orderlies in the asylum wing of the hospital!"

It was going down fast, and about to get physical. I had to jump into the middle of it. I shouted at the top of my lungs, "Fucking knock it off, the two of you! Mum, go home! I will call you later. You! Stop this shit!" My mother walked off and we headed home.

The first half of the day was finished – round one. Now for round two. She raged on and on. "How dare she talk to you like that! Putting her walking stick in your face!" I told her I was not worried about that shit, and I was going to the phone box. She would not let me go without her being there to listen to the conversation. The fighting went on for hours.

When she had finally quieted down a bit, late in the day, we went out and I made the call. My mother answered my hello with "I never thought you would call." I asked her what was going on. She answered, "I'm not going to apologise to her or you after today's outburst." I told her I would come to visit her soon. She said, "Not if she is going to be there!" and slammed down the phone.

Time for round three.

After my mother hung up, my flatmate began again. "How dare she say that I can't be there! She knows how well I have looked after you!" I had had enough. "I don't care anymore! Stop this crazy talk! I just want to go home to my bed and sleep off this horrible day." She was silent as we walked home.

Once we were inside, did she carry on! She was still going at 3:36am. She threw in everything she could think of for good measure. "How dare she do this! How dare she do that! I am going around to her house to smash her face in, just like I should of when that slut who wanted to fuck you asked you for a light! I am going to call my biker friends to sort this out!" I begged her to stop all this wild talk. She responded by picking up a dinner plate and throwing it at my head.

I managed to put up my left arm and block it. The plate shattered, and a large shard broke off and went deep into my arm. I looked down, saw the chunk of white china hanging there and turned to show her what she had done. She just watched the blood running down my arm. "What do you want me to do about it?" she said. "Don't you feel bad for doing this to me?" I asked. She looked me right in the eyes. "No. I don't feel bad. You are as stupid as your mother, you backward fuck!"

I pulled out the shard. Blood was running everywhere. I took off my t-shirt and wrapped it around the wound to stop the bleeding. I walked off and cleaned up my arm in the bathroom then went to bed. I did not want to see her face again; not after she did that to me.

I write again

The two of you would have been a good match if I had let you both go at it

My flat mate and my mother. Ding, ding! Round one! Let the fight begin!

The both of you had dirty mouths and played dirty games

No matter how many rounds you had, you would still try and play me

Mother: Come home! I love you! Flat mate: Don't listen! She will hurt you!

Flat mate: She does not love you. She is only trying to control you.

Mother: Your ex-girlfriend has had a baby now and it looks like you.

Flat mate: Remember the hose she used on you, the pain and scars.

Mother: She is trying to turn you against us. Listen to me, or you're not my son anymore.